—

PLACE YOUR PHOTO HERE.

I dedicate my journal to

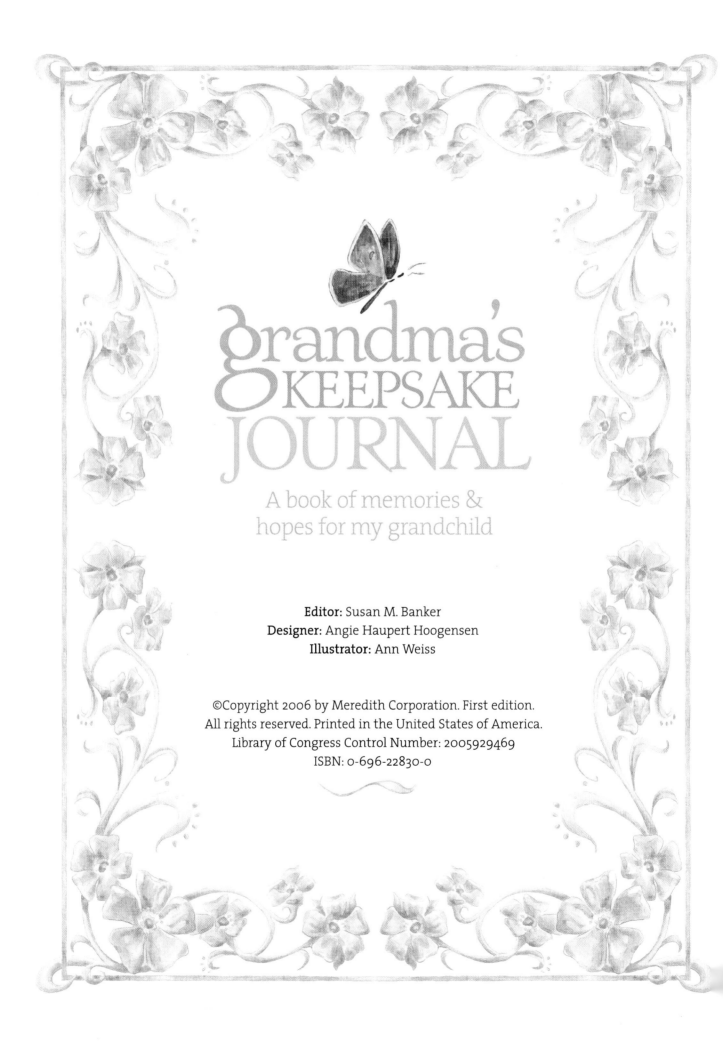

grandma's KEEPSAKE JOURNAL

A book of memories &
hopes for my grandchild

Editor: Susan M. Banker
Designer: Angie Haupert Hoogensen
Illustrator: Ann Weiss

©Copyright 2006 by Meredith Corporation. First edition.
All rights reserved. Printed in the United States of America.
Library of Congress Control Number: 2005929469
ISBN: 0-696-22830-0

contents

sweet memories of *yesterday*

I love to think of days gone by,
of friends so dear and family ties.
It's the people I've known
and the places I've been
that make this Grandma
who I am.

PLACE A COPY OF YOUR BIRTH CERTIFICATE HERE.

I was born on _____ in the city of _____

to my proud parents, _____

I weighed _____ and measured _____

My delivery was _____

_____

_____

_____

yesterday

People tell me that as a baby I looked like _____

_____

_____

When I was an infant, we lived _____

_____

_____

Our home was _____

_____

_____

PLACE YOUR BABY PHOTO HERE.

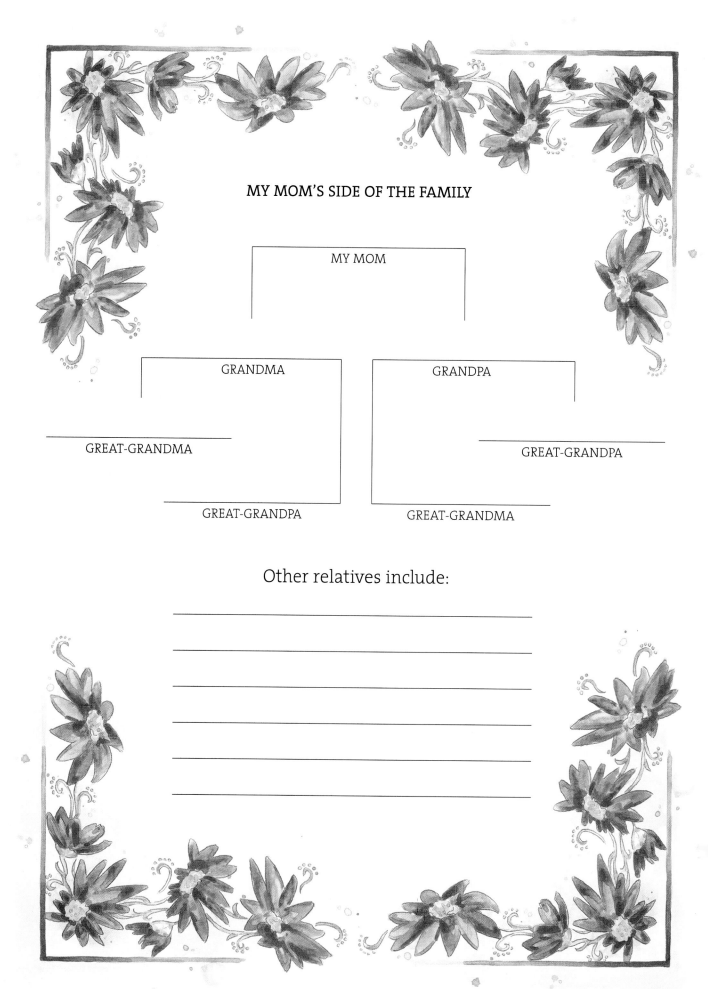

MY MOM'S SIDE OF THE FAMILY

MY MOM

GRANDMA

GRANDPA

GREAT-GRANDMA

GREAT-GRANDPA

GREAT-GRANDPA

GREAT-GRANDMA

Other relatives include:

_____

_____

_____

_____

_____

_____

yesterday

I called my **mom** _____

Her maiden name was _____

Mom was born in _____

She grew up in _____

She and dad married _____

I called my **grandma** _____

Her maiden name was _____

Grandma was born in _____

She grew up in _____

She and grandpa married _____

I called my **grandpa** _____

Grandpa was born in _____

He grew up in _____

Ancestors from my mom's side came from _____

_____

_____

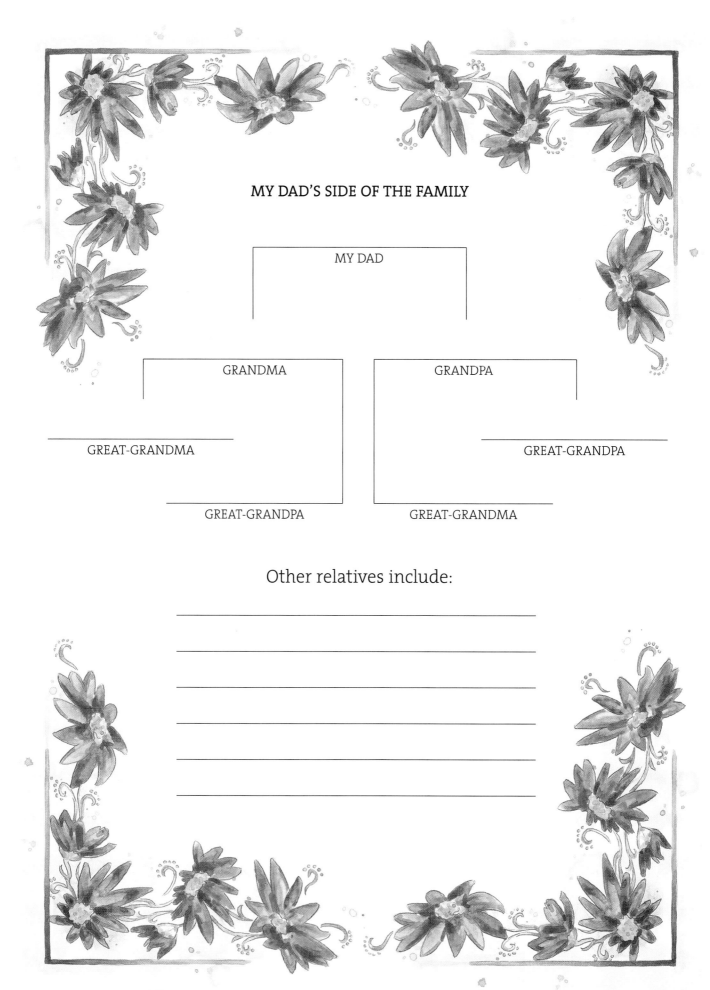

MY DAD'S SIDE OF THE FAMILY

MY DAD

GRANDMA

GRANDPA

GREAT-GRANDMA

GREAT-GRANDPA

GREAT-GRANDPA

GREAT-GRANDMA

Other relatives include:

_____

_____

_____

_____

_____

_____

yesterday

I called my **dad** _____

Dad was born in _____

He grew up in _____

I called my **grandma** _____

Her maiden name was _____

Grandma was born in _____

She grew up in _____

She and grandpa married _____

I called my **grandpa** _____

Grandpa was born in _____

He grew up in _____

Ancestors from my dad's side came from

_____

_____

_____

_____

When I was a **little** I loved to _____

_____

_____

_____

My favorite toy was _____

_____

_____

My playmates were _____

_____

_____

When my parents went out, I had a babysitter named _____

_____

_____

My first word was _____

_____

I got my first tooth _____

_____

I lost my first tooth _____

_____

I learned to ride a bike _____

_____

_____

yesterday

I started **school** when I was _____

_____

The name of my elementary school was _____

_____

_____

My kindergarten teacher's name was _____

_____

My favorite time at school was _____

_____

_____

_____

My best subject was _____

_____

_____

_____

I wasn't very good at _____

_____

_____

_____

I changed **schools** when I was _____

_____

_____

My favorite classes were _____

_____

_____

My grades were usually _____

_____

_____

One teacher who stands out above the rest is _____

_____

_____

If my parents couldn't find me I was usually _____

_____

_____

My school chums were _____

_____

_____

I got really nervous in school when _____

_____

_____

yesterday

When I was a **teenager**, I lived for _____

_____

_____

_____

My parents got mad at me when I _____

_____

_____

_____

My friends looked to me for _____

_____

_____

_____

My curfew was _____

_____

_____

I learned to drive _____

_____

_____

My most memorable **high school** moment was _____

_____

_____

_____

I'll never forget my most embarrassing time in school when I _____

_____

_____

_____

If my yearbook would have had a spot for it, I would have been

named the most likely to _____

_____

_____

_____

My favorite thing to wear to school was _____

_____

_____

_____

I still keep in touch with these school

friends _____

_____

_____

_____

My favorite **graduation** memories are

_____

_____

_____

_____

_____

_____

PLACE HIGH SCHOOL PHOTO
OR A COPY OF A DIPLOMA, REPORT CARD,
OR OTHER SCHOOL DOCUMENT HERE.

After high school I _____

_____

_____

_____

My biggest hope at that time was _____

_____

_____

I really tried hard to _____

_____

_____

To get around I _____

_____

_____

I lived _____

_____

_____

I wish I had devoted more time to _____

_____

_____

_____

_____

_____

My **first job** was _____

_____

_____

_____

I made about $ _____ an hour to do such duties as _____

_____

_____

After that I learned to _____

_____

_____

Other jobs I had included _____

_____

_____

The place I liked working the most was _____

_____

_____

_____

When I met **my husband**-to-be we were _____

_____

_____

He was _____

_____

_____

I couldn't believe he _____

_____

_____

_____

What I liked best about him was _____

_____

_____

_____

_____

He told me _____

_____

_____

_____

_____

yesterday

We **dated** for _____

_____

Our favorite thing to do was _____

_____

_____

_____

The things we had in common were _____

_____

_____

_____

The one thing we differed on was _____

_____

_____

He asked me to marry him on _____

_____

_____

_____

I **married Grandpa** on _____

_____

_____

The wedding was held at _____

_____

_____

I wore _____

_____

_____

_____

_____

Your grandpa wore _____

_____

_____

The guest list included _____

_____

_____

_____

Our reception was _____

_____

_____

_____

PLACE YOUR WEDDING PHOTO HERE.

When I look at this photo I

_____

_____

_____

_____

_____

_____

After we were **married**, we honeymooned _____

_____

_____

_____

_____

Our first home together was _____

_____

_____

_____

_____

Friends and family who visited us were _____

_____

_____

_____

_____

We loved to get away to _____

_____

_____

_____

_____

_____

yesterday

The thought of starting **our own family** was _____

_____

_____

_____

_____

I became pregnant _____

_____

I gave birth to _____ on _____

_____

_____

_____

Other children included _____

_____

_____

_____

_____

_____

_____

My **health** throughout the years has been _____

_____

_____

_____

_____

The time I remember hurting the most was _____

_____

_____

_____

_____

I thought I was going to die when _____

_____

_____

_____

_____

Just in case it runs in families, I have _____

_____

_____

_____

_____

yesterday

I was in the **hospital** when _____

_____

_____

_____

As far as surgeries go, I've had _____

_____

_____

_____

I have a scar on my _____

_____

_____

_____

My worst accident was _____

_____

_____

_____

_____

_____

Looking back, I wouldn't trade _____

_____

_____

_____

_____

If I had to pick a favorite year, it would be _____

_____

_____

_____

_____

The year I'd like to forget was _____

_____

_____

_____

_____

I'll always remember traveling to _____

_____

_____

_____

_____

_____

PLACE A FAVORITE YESTERYEAR PHOTO HERE.

This photo means a lot to me because

_____

_____

_____

_____

_____

_____

joyful wonders of *today*

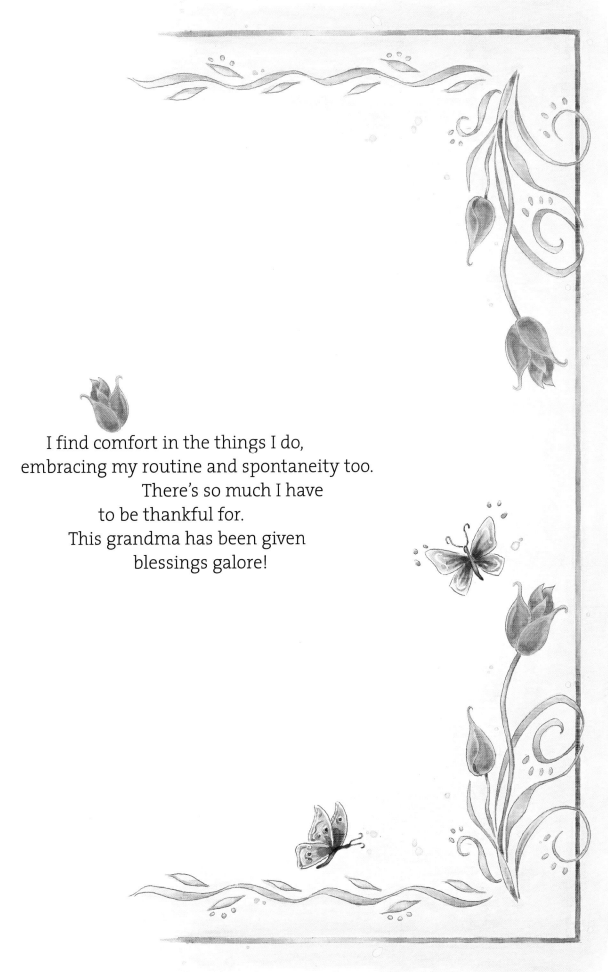

I find comfort in the things I do,
embracing my routine and spontaneity too.
There's so much I have
to be thankful for.
This grandma has been given
blessings galore!

I currently **live** at _____

_____

_____

_____

My home is _____

_____

_____

_____

The city where I live is _____

The best part about living here is _____

_____

_____

I like to shop at _____

_____

_____

_____

_____

I often attend the _____

_____

_____

_____

_____

PLACE A PHOTO OF HOME HERE.

I **moved** here because

_____

_____

_____

_____

_____

_____

My **daily routine** consists of _____

_____

_____

_____

_____

I usually get up at _____ o'clock and go to bed at _____

_____

I take these medicines _____

_____

_____

It's a bonus when I get to _____

_____

_____

I always try to make time for _____

_____

_____

There never seems to be enough time for _____

_____

_____

_____

_____

today

It **makes my day** to talk on the phone to _____

_____

I love getting letters from _____

_____

I enjoy the television show _____

_____

If I had to choose just one kind of music to

listen to, it would be _____

_____

My favorite singer or group is _____

_____

I subscribe to _____

_____

I enjoy reading _____

_____

I love the sport of _____

_____

_____

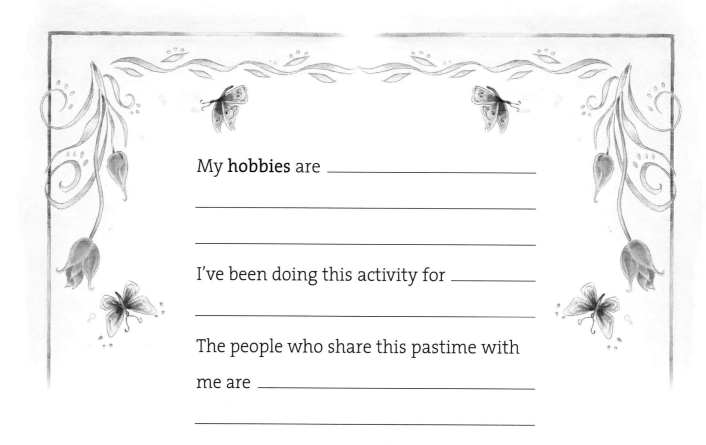

My **hobbies** are _____

_____

_____

I've been doing this activity for _____

_____

The people who share this pastime with

me are _____

_____

PLACE A PHOTO OF YOU ENJOYING A HOBBY HERE.

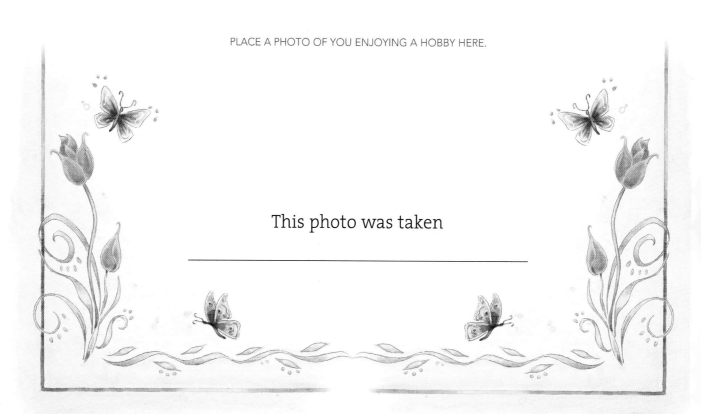

This photo was taken

_____

today

My **religious beliefs** are _____

_____

_____

_____

_____

_____

_____

_____

_____

_____

I attend this church _____

_____

_____

My favorite religious passage is _____

_____

_____

_____

_____

Throughout the year I make a point to **visit these relatives** _____

_____

_____

_____

_____

_____

Family members who visit me most often include _____

_____

_____

_____

_____

_____

Here are some addresses I want to be sure you have _____

_____

_____

_____

_____

_____

_____

_____

_____

today.

PLACE A FAMILY PHOTO HERE.

This photo was taken on _____

PLACE A PHOTO OF YOU AND
YOUR GRANDCHILD HERE.

This photo of us was taken on _____

Friends I treasure the most include _____

_____

_____

_____

My friends and I like to _____

_____

_____

_____

PLACE A PHOTO OF YOU AND A FRIEND HERE.

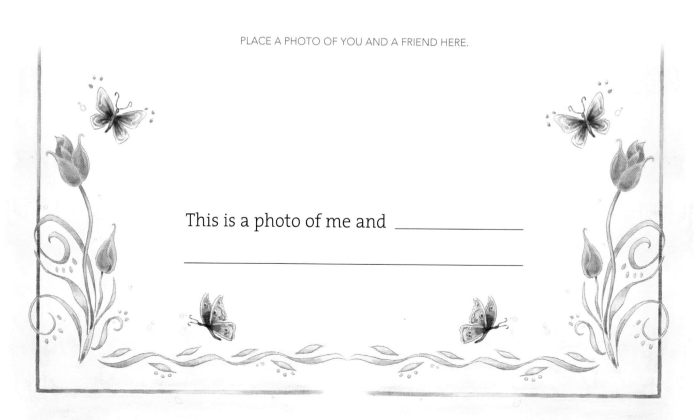

This is a photo of me and _____

_____

My favorite **food** to eat is _____

_____

_____

_____

_____

It's a treat to go to the restaurant _____

_____

_____

_____

When I indulge in dessert, I order _____

_____

_____

_____

I wouldn't mind if I never had to eat _____

_____

_____

_____

Specialty foods **I cook** include _____

_____

_____

_____

_____

The recipe of mine that you like the most is _____

_____

_____

Here it is, so you can pass it on _____

_____

_____

_____

_____

_____

_____

_____

_____

_____

_____

_____

_____

_____

These tried-and-true **recipes** have been in our family for generations

_____

_____

_____

_____

_____

_____

_____

_____

_____

_____

_____

_____

_____

In my opinion, the best part of the

newspaper is _____

_____

_____

PLACE A NEWSPAPER CLIPPING HERE.

These **comic strips** make me laugh _____

_____

_____

_____

_____

_____

_____

PLACE COMIC STRIP HERE.

PLACE COMIC STRIP HERE.

Here are more of **my favorites**:

Color _____

Flower _____

Scent _____

Number _____

Animal _____

Actor _____

Actress _____

Movie _____

Style of art _____

Fashion accessory _____

Car _____

Board game _____

Card game _____

Holiday _____

Bird _____

Beverage _____

Mode of transportation _____

Season _____

State _____

today

PLACE YOUR DRAWING HERE.

Here's my best effort in drawing a **self-portrait**.

sincere *t* wishes for *tomorrow*

I've seen many changes
          in the days gone by,
from cars on the road to
          the flavors of pie.
               I wonder what's ahead for
          this big, wide world?
     I'll bet it'll be different
          than when I was a girl!

My **secret wish** for you is _____

_____

_____

_____

_____

_____

_____

_____

I'd love it if you could _____

_____

_____

_____

_____

_____

I believe you have what it takes to _____

_____

_____

_____

_____

_____

_____

tomorrow

If **wishing** would make it so, I'd live _____

_____

_____

My dream vacation is _____

_____

_____

_____

If I could have any job it would be _____

_____

_____

_____

The one person I'd give anything to meet is _____

_____

_____

If I won the lottery, I would _____

_____

_____

_____

_____

_____

The thing I'd like to **change** about me is _____

_____

_____

_____

_____

What I wouldn't give to look like _____

_____

_____

_____

_____

If I could exchange a body part for a new one, it would be

_____

_____

_____

If calories were of no concern, I'd make a meal out of _____

_____

_____

_____

_____

tomorrow

When I dream about a **perfect world**, I wish I could _____

_____

_____

_____

_____

I often worry about _____

_____

_____

_____

_____

Life's too short to _____

_____

_____

_____

_____

_____

I hope you'll carry on some of these

family traditions _____

_____

_____

_____

_____

_____

_____

_____

_____

_____

_____

_____

_____

_____

_____

_____

_____

_____

tomorrow

I give to the following **charities** _____

_____

_____

Because _____

_____

_____

Because _____

_____

_____

Because _____

_____

_____

Here are some grandmotherly **words of advice** _____

tomorrow

Some uplifting **sayings** to remember as you look to tomorrow

PLACE CLIPPING HERE.

PLACE CLIPPING HERE.

_____

_____

_____

PLACE CLIPPING HERE.

_____

_____

_____

_____

_____

_____

_____

_____

Remember that each new day is a gift—an opportunity to do **good things** with your life, such as _____

_____

_____

_____

_____

_____

_____

As you choose your friends and companions, look for these characteristics _____

_____

_____

_____

_____

I'm always happy to meet someone who _____

_____

_____

_____

_____

tomorrow

Believe in the power of **prayer** because _____

_____

_____

_____

My most heartfelt prayers include _____

_____

_____

_____

_____

_____

If just one of my prayers could be answered tomorrow,

it would be _____

_____

_____

_____

_____

On my next **birthday**, I hope I _____

_____

_____

On your next birthday, I hope _____

_____

_____

I'd love to make you a cake in the shape of _____

_____

_____

The gift I'd like to give you the most is _____

_____

_____

If we celebrate our birthdays together, I'd love to take you to _____

_____

_____

I wish tomorrow would be a **beautiful day** like this one

PLACE A PHOTO HERE.

This photo was taken on

_____

_____

_____

_____

_____

_____

things to remember always

We're granted many joys
       mixed with sorrows along the way.
    It's a blending of experiences—
life's curtain call of plays.
        So let's recall the very most
     important of all these.
    They're the fabric of our existence
     in this loving family.

Here are some **special dates** to remember _____

_____
_____
_____
_____
_____
_____
_____
_____
_____
_____
_____
_____
_____
_____
_____
_____
_____
_____

PLACE A PHOTO OF YOU AND YOUR GRANDCHILD HERE.

This was a **special day** for us, remember? We were

_____

_____

_____

_____

Grandma-isms and other wonderful sayings

I want you to remember _____

_____

_____

_____

_____

_____

_____

_____

_____

_____

_____

_____

_____

_____

_____

always

These are the words to my **favorite song** _____

_____

_____

_____

_____

_____

_____

_____

_____

_____

_____

_____

_____

_____

_____

I love this **poem** _____

_____

_____

_____

_____

_____

_____

_____

_____

_____

_____

_____

_____

_____

_____

_____

_____

_____

Of all my **accomplishments**, I am most proud of

_____

_____

_____

_____

_____

_____

_____

My biggest **regret** in life is _____

_____

_____

_____

_____

_____

I hope you'll **never forget** _____

_____

_____

_____

_____

_____

_____

_____

_____

_____

_____

_____

_____

_____

_____

_____

_____

_____

My final words of **wisdom** _____

_____

_____

_____

_____

_____

_____

_____

_____

_____

_____

_____

_____

_____

TREASURED PHOTOS

These **photos** are dear to my heart, just as you are. Treasure and enjoy them always.

always

TREASURED PHOTOS

always

FAMILY RECORDS

These certificates, licenses, and other mementos will help you remember our **family history**.

always

FAMILY RECORDS

always

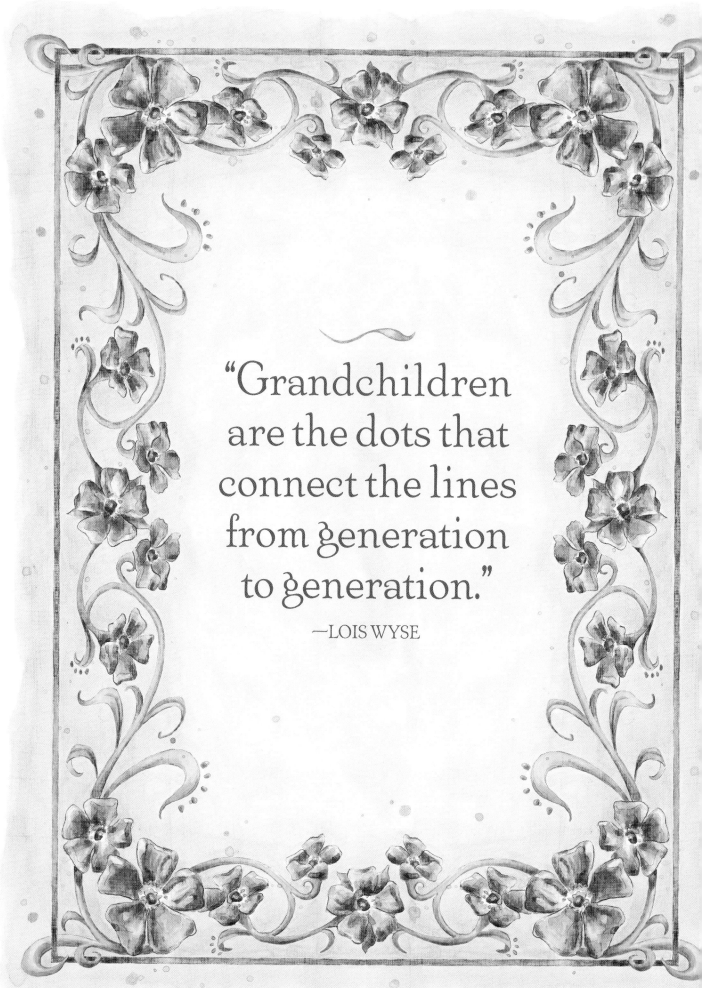

"Grandchildren
are the dots that
connect the lines
from generation
to generation."

—LOIS WYSE